SPRINGS AND FOUNTAINS OF LIFE

THE
CORNERSTONE
PUBLISHING

31 Keys to Successful Living

OLATUNJI J. OGUNBANJO

SPRINGS AND FOUNTAINS OF LIFE
31 Keys to Successful Living

Cornerstone Publishing
A Division of Cornerstone Creativity Group LLC
Phone: +1(516) 547-4999
info@thecornerstonepublishers.com
www.thecornerstonepublishers.com

To order bulk copies of this book or to contact the author please call +1781-346-8085 or email: olaclaim@gmail.com

DEDICATION

This book is specially dedicated to my Angels - Ibukun, Shalom, and Folakemi.

ACKNOWLEDGMENTS

First and foremost my profound gratitude goes to Almighty God, the Creator of Heaven and Earth who granted me victory and success in life, and also for His gifts of the Holy Spirit in me. Thank you Lord!

Thanks to these God's generals: Rev Bunmi Olusola of Diadem Christian Church, Ijebu-Ode, Rev M. Olatunde Dairo, Bishop Francis Wale Oke, Bishop Olumuyiwa Ojo, Bishop Julius Abiola, Pastor James Taiwo, Pastor Shola Jordan Adeoye, Pastor Dr M.O. Babalola, Pastor Titus Joshua Oluwasuyi, and all member of CAC Mount Zion II. Lynn.

Special thanks also goes to my family, all members of CLAIM worldwide, Prophetess Olayinka Olabisi, Pastor Seyi Hopewell, Mrs. Abiola Kadiri, Mrs. Olaide Oshibogun and others too numerous to mention. And lastly my hearty appreciation goes to Pastor Gbenga Showunmi of The Cornerstone Publishing, a dynamic man of God who made this dream possible a reality in publishing this book. Thank you very much and God bless you all!

CONTENTS

INTRODUCTION

"And I will give you the keys of the kingdom of heaven: and whatsoever thou shalt bind on earth shall be bound in heaven and whatsoever thou shalt loose on earth shall be loosed in heaven" (Matthew 16:19).

In this book, you will discover the keys that unlock destinies. God's plan for your life entails thoughts of peace, hope, and a good future so you will live successfully every day (Jeremiah 29:11). How do I know that? The Word of God says the path of the righteous shines and shines eternally (Proverbs 4:18).

These daily devotions are capsules to be taken each day of the month for your entire life. You are bound to be a success as you apply the principles contained herein. To enjoy the full benefits of this devotional, you must obey the fundamental truths shared in it. Just read one topic a day and you are through.

Reading these topics continually will form good habits in your life for success. A major pathway to success is to program your daily life and regularly engage in positive things that will evolve later as accomplishments. Working, saving money, studying, investing, tithing, saying early morning prayers and affirmations, paying your bills promptly, weekly fasting and thorough preparation before you do anything will produce success.

There is a story of a wealthy man who had only one son. In an attempt to make the child independent and succeed after the death of the rich man, he gave the son a bag full of money and a little book. He then asked the son to go very far to a country he wished, start his own life without interferences and make sure he spent the money wisely to be wealthy too. So that after ten years, if he was successful, the rich man will be glad he has a son who will carry on his wealth and spend it wisely.

Lo and behold, the son took the big bag of money and the little book and went his way. He got to the city he liked, started a business he liked, and continue spending and investing based on the way people in the city were doing.

At the end of nine and a half years, all the money was reduced to a few notes due to his inexperience, no knowledge or wisdom and failure to understand the principles of life and finances. One day, he sat down in his room and remembered the bag his father gave him and saw the little book untouched for over nine and a half years. He picked it up and started reading. What was inside the book? The book contained principles of life on how to spend the money in the big bag profitably and how to be fruitful and multiply the money every year.

The son started crying lamenting that he had wasted all his money over those years struggling to make it instead of just sitting down for a few minutes to understand the principles of life before venturing into the unknown world. He then picked up the few dollars he had left and started all over to follow the principles in the book his father gave him.

Dear readers, most of us are like this young man. We dabble into the world thinking we can succeed without learning. This is a powerful principle book that can be used to form godly habits for success (Proverbs 10:22). The power and secrets revealed in it are consistent. They will explore how to live your life and be successful. Buy the truth and sell it not. It is the application of the principles of God in your life that will make you prosperous. These principles are the habits you must form to build you up to have success in life. Naturally, there are keys to open different doors. Likewise, there are also keys that open doors for successful living.

The keys shared here are divine secrets and mysteries that God has planned for our lives to prosper. You have to align yourself with these keys, principles, and God to have total success. Read a chapter of the book of Proverbs in the Bible daily as given in this book. As you do that, you will succeed. Remain blessed forever.

1
WORSHIP AND SERVE GOD

"Hear O Israel: the Lord our God is one Lord: and thou shalt love the Lord thy God with all thine heart, and with all thy soul, and with all thy might" *(Deuteronomy 6:4-5).*

To serve God effectively, you must be saved and born again. Your soul's salvation is very important in this life and in the world to come. For you to fully enjoy the success and blessings of God, you must be born again.

"Jesus answered, verily, verily, I say unto thee, except a man be born of water and of the Spirit, he cannot enter into the kingdom of God" (John 3:3).

As you grow with God, you have to understand your position in Christ (Ephesians 2:6, Ephesians 1:21) and exercise your authority as a believer (Mark 16:15).

It is in the process of worshipping God that you receive breakthroughs, deliverance, and blessings. Serving God is more about being available to do the works of God than just attending church. The more you serve God, the better things will work according to your plans.

Action Point:

Read and meditate on Proverbs 1

Take a decision to do something in the house of God at least weekly

2
DEPART FROM INIQUITY

At the foundation of your life and one of the first things you should do is to depart from iniquity. This is spiritual cleansing to prepare you for the blessings of God. God loves you and He desires the best for you. If you are not clean, you cannot have the best of God.

"If you return to the Almighty, you will be built up; you will remove iniquity far from your tents. Then you will lay your gold in the dust, and the gold of Ophir among the stones of the brooks" (Job 22:23-24).

"Nevertheless the solid foundation of God stands, having this seal: 'The Lord knows those who are His, and let everyone who names the name of Christ depart from iniquity'" (2 Timothy 2:19)

I visited a church in New York City where I saw a man of God preaching. In his preaching, he told us a story about when he was an unbeliever in the world. He was a leader of a drug pushing group throughout the States. But he got to a point when he cried to God and said, "God, I got money; I don't know what to do with it." He got in contact with some great men of God who prayed for him, and he was delivered. He repented, turned around, and gave his life to God. Since that time, he has been on the move for God. When he was arrested and tried for various offences, he told the judge that he was sorry and now he is living for Jesus. The judge was angry but said he had seen a new man in this pastor, and he could not send him back to jail to be in a worse position after repentance; he was set free. He is now living happily and successfully without having to run away from the law enforcement agents.

"An unexamined life is not worth living" — Socrates

Action Point:

Read and meditate on Proverbs 2

Think and consider your ways. Make a decision today to drop a sin from your life

3
FORGIVE OTHERS

Forgiveness is a hardcore principle that people find difficult to do. However, if you are able to forgive others, it removes bitterness, anger, and hatred. It also makes room for quick answers to your prayers. On the other hand, unforgiveness blocks answers to your prayers. You have to forgive others to move ahead in life.

"And forgive us our trespasses, as we forgive those who trespass against us" (Matthew 6:12).

"Let all bitterness, wrath, anger, clamor, and evil speaking be put away from you, with all malice. And be kind to one another, tenderhearted, forgiving one another, even as God in Christ forgave you" (Ephesians 4:31-32).

"The Weak can never forgive. Forgiveness is the attitude of the strong" —Mahatma Gandhi

A great man of God was praying for a very sick man in a wheelchair. The man of God wanted to lay his hands on the sick man but the Holy Spirit told him not to do so until the sick man confessed his sins. He told the sick man what the Holy Spirit said but the sick man replied that he had no unconfessed sins in his life. The pastor through the Holy Spirit then told him that he had not forgiven his ex-wife who left him many years before. The sick man later agreed, confessed the sin and forgave his former wife in his heart. Immediately after his genuine confession and forgiveness, he was instantly and miraculously healed by the Holy Spirit. That is the power of forgiveness.

If you are yet to have breakthroughs in any areas of your life, examine your life to see if you are harboring unforgiveness or sin. Unforgiveness blocks answers to prayers. As you forgive others God will answer all your prayers.

You have to forgive others so that God can forgive you. Unforgiveness creates bitterness, hatred, and anger in our lives and does not allow us to focus on what's important. Unforgiveness is a distraction.

Action Point:

Read and meditate on Proverbs 3

- Write out a list of all those people who offend you and forgive them in your heart

- Write out a list of all those you offend and ask God to forgive you

4
BE LED BY THE HOLY SPIRIT

Before you can be led by the Holy Spirit, you must receive Him into your spirit. Ask God to release His Spirit inside of you, and you will receive Him.

Receiving the Holy Spirit is necessary for you to be anointed and always led by Him. It takes faith to obey the Spirit in this material world. We are spirit-beings who have to listen and hear from the Spirit of God. "God is a Spirit, and they that worship Him must worship Him in Spirit and in truth" (John 4:24). Therefore, He has given us the Holy Spirit to lead, guide, and talk to us.

"For as many as are led by the Spirit of God, these are the sons of God" (Romans 8:14).

The best directions we can receive as believers come from the Holy Spirit. God promises to instruct us and teach us the way we should go. If you want to be successful, you must be Spirit- led.

I like to work, move, and minister under the direction and unction of the Holy Spirit. Most of my writings, preaching, and actions are inspired by Him especially when I am alone and meditating. As I begin to receive, so I write. The more I write, the more I receive. What you get under the inspiration of the Holy Spirit is more genuine and authentic, and it will last forever. Be inspired by the Holy Spirit. Receive from Him and work on whatever He says. Do not move until you hear from Him. Let the Spirit guide, guard, and direct you for life. If you can be patient enough to listen and obey the Holy Spirit daily, your life will be meaningful.

"We cannot effectively serve God without the Holy Spirit" —Derek Prince

Action Point:

Read and meditate on Proverbs 4

• Kneel down and ask God Almighty to

release His Spirit upon you now.

- Take a decision to always be sensitive to the voice of the Holy Spirit and obey.

5
DELIVER THYSELF

It was my spiritual father who taught me the principle of delivering oneself. Dr. D.K Olukoya of Mountain of Fire and Miracles Ministries also wrote a book on when a deliverer needs deliverance. I believe in depending on normal Christian living but when the enemies did not stop attacking me, I had to fight back seriously.

At each point of our lives, we all need deliverance daily, weekly or monthly. So for you to have progressive success each day, you need periodic deliverance. Deliverance is an art of regular spiritual checkups of your life. It is also a time to cast out the fiery darts of the enemies. It is a time of spiritual warfare.

"So do this my son, and deliver yourself…Deliver yourself like a gazelle from the hand of the hunter; and a bird from the hand of the fowler" (Proverbs 6:3a, 5).

Deliverance is a deliberate act of praying and separating yourself from evildoers. You begin by pleading the blood of Jesus to cover you and your loved ones. You set the bloodline. You set yourself free. You destroy the works of the enemies (1 John 3:8.) You cleanse yourself and cut off any entanglements and encroachments from your life. You silence the enemies. You break any evil cords and ancestral covenants in your life, marriage, destiny, and ministry.

Why periodic deliverance? You need to do this because we are in this world but not of this world. This world is full of evildoers, corrupt practices, demons, and evil spirits that are moving about, touching you without you knowing it. Also, unknown forces and attacks are on the rampage flying over everywhere with their toxicities. In the course of your daily routine and work, you are bound to encounter unclean persons with negative radiation that needs to be cleansed and delivered from your body and life.

Somewhere in South America, a live wall gecko was cast out of a sister after an intensive deliverance session. It was a surprising one. That was what the Enemy planted in her that was disturbing her destiny and delaying her progress in life. After the deliverance, things began to work speedily and positively for her. Praise God!

In the process of deliverance, you bind, cast out, cast down every imagination, and uproot every stronghold out of any areas of your life. Send them to the abyss, the bottomless pit. Total deliverance, removing the evil plantations of the enemies, and removing household enemies/foundational problems require continuous prayers.

Action Point:

Read and meditate on Proverbs 5

Take an entire day to seriously fast and pray to break off any negativity attached to your life.

6
HAVE MENTORS

The first mentor you can have is the Holy Spirit. Then you also need a human mentor. Mentors are your guides in the journey of your life. There are some people that God has put ahead of us with positive experiences who are ready to put us through and make our journeys in this world easier. Seek those in your field and area of interest to follow. You can follow them through books, tapes, videos, and contacts. Mentors are directors of your life.

Mentoring is a process of having a physical guide in life. This is someone on your path of purpose who knows a lot and has gone ahead of you. He/she is willing to teach and guide you aright so that you will not fall into the mistakes of life. Mentoring is a smooth way of reaching the top without fear.

"His mother said to the servants, whatever He says to you, do it" (John 2:5).

You have to get the heart to follow whatever your mentor tells you. Bishop David Oyedepo is a mentor to Rev Sam Adeyemi, while Kenneth Copeland is a Mentor to Creflo Dollar. John Maxwell is a mentor to many leaders throughout the world. You too can get your own mentor in your field. "To mold your life, you need someone to scold you in life."

"Tell me and I forget, teach me and I may remember, involve me and I learn" —Benjamin Franklin

Action Point:

Read and meditate on Proverbs 6

Connect with a Mentor related to your purpose in life and begin to follow the person through books, tapes, the internet and if possible direct contact

7
PRAYING TONGUES

Praying in tongues is praying in the language of God. It is a more aright pray than praying in your own language (understanding). Praying in tongues is a divine secret that God gives us to overcome situations, challenges, and have victory in life. But because our minds usually want to know and understand everything in the language we speak, we tend to stop praying in tongues and do it our own way. There are many benefits of praying or speaking in tongues. The more you pray in tongues, the more you are on the right path to your destiny of successful living. However, if you are yet to speak in tongues, don't despair, ask God (Luke 11:13).

"For he who speaks in a tongue does not speak to men but to God, for no man understands him; however, in the spirit, he speaks mysteries" (1 Corinthians 14:2)

"He who speaks in a tongue edifies himself, but he who prophesies edifies the church" (1 Corinthians 14:4).

"For if I pray in a tongue, my spirit prays, but my understanding is unfruitful" (1 Corinthians 14:14).

Speaking in tongues is the supernatural language of God. It is refreshing, powerful, and helps us to pray the will of God for our lives and others. It is a secret and mystery from God. Praying a lot in tongues will give you more spiritual power.

"I am living and having supernatural experiences. A lot of people get really freaked out about that; I speak in tongues; I have been baptized in the Holy Spirit" —Stephen Baldwin

A woman of God in the USA changed her praying from the natural language to the spiritual language of praying in tongues for several hours some days. The results were unexpected miracles and miraculous reactions. Even her son commented that he did not even know what was happening in their home. That is the power of God in action.

When you pray in tongues your spirit in conjunction with the Holy Spirit will help you to pray aright because most times, we don't know how to pray. Speaking in tongues is inspired by the Holy Spirit; you can speak, pray, talk or sing in tongues. Praying in tongues is a spiritual incantation that makes all things work together for your good.

Action Point:

Read and meditate on Proverbs 7

- Pray in tongues for three hours a day.
- Ask for the gift of praying in tongues.

8
MEDITATE ON THE WORD

This is a secret to success in life. Meditation is an act of thinking, muttering and saying words to yourself while you are available for direction from heaven. It is in the process of meditation that inspiration will come with ideas and what to do next as a decision. Meditating on the Word of God is essential.

"This Book of the Law shall not depart from your mouth, but you shall meditate in it day and night, that you may observe to do according to all that is written in it. For then you will make your way prosperous, and then you will have good success" (Joshua 1:8).

"But his delight is in the law of the Lord, and in His Law he meditates day and night. He shall be like a tree planted by the rivers of water that brings forth its fruits in its season, whose leaf also shall not wither, and whatever he does prosper" (Psalms 1:2-3).

The more you meditate, the better the ideas

and inspiration you will receive and the more help will come your way. All things will begin to work together for your good. Do not jump into anything in life without clear meditation.

"Meditation practice isn't about trying to throw ourselves away and become something better, it's about befriending who we are" — Ani Pema Chodron

The best way to meditate is on the Word of God. Biblical meditation means filling your mind with the truth of God's Word. A great man of God said, "Many of us want a word from the Lord but we refused to pick a word from His Word – Bible." In meditation, you are to pick a verse of the scripture that pertains to the situation at hand. Read it to yourself; mutter it to yourself believing it and allowing the Word to sink inside you so you can perform the miraculous.

The more you meditate, the more you will be inspired, and the more all things will work together in your favor.

How to Meditate

• First, breathe in and out.

- Then relax your body from head to toes.

- Sit in a quiet comfortable place you like.

- Think about your specific request.

- Pick a scripture that goes with your request.

- Silently and gently repeat the scripture to yourself and to your spirit.

- Repeat it for as long as you want.

- Then stop, relax, and release yourself.

I published a small book titled, *You Must Meditate Day and Night* sometime ago. I gave a copy to a woman of God. She read it quickly and began to read the book daily into her spirit. Within a few days, doors of opportunities began to open to her. She was surprised that the meditation book could work that way. She bought some and gave to her loved ones and members of her church.

The Spirit of God will bring your request (1 Corinthians 2:11).

A real man must create time to meditate. If you have no time to meditate, you are slowing down your progress.

Action Point:

Read and meditate on Proverbs 8.

- Think about the situation you are going through now.

- Locate a bible verse related to the issues.

- Read the bible verse slowly over and over to yourself for as long as you can.

9
FAST REGULARLY

Fasting is a willing abstinence or reduction from some or all kinds of food, drinks or both for a period of time. Fasting makes you light, free and allows you to easily get connected to God. There are many benefits of fasting as the Bible teaches us. One of them is that it will connect you easily with the supernatural giving you an edge over the physical realms, giving you victory, and allowing you to do exploits in life. You get many things done easily at the supernatural level. You need to apply fasting to your life periodically and be prepared to connect to God, do His will, and fulfill your destiny.

"Start the practice of self-control with some penance; begin with fasting"—Mahavira

Fasting adds spiritual power to your life. The more you fast, the more you are empowered.

You don't have to be too heavy to pray, think, meditate or to receive inspiration. Fasting allows the flow of the anointing to heal, bless, and minister. It is the spiritual that controls the physical. Fasting prepares you to be spiritual.

"Everyone can perform magic, everyone can reach his goals, if he is able to wait, if he is able to fast." —Hermann Hesse

"So He said unto them, 'this kind can come out by nothing but by prayer and fasting'" (Mark 9:29).

There are some issues in your destiny to which you have to apply fasting and prayer before you can make headway. But the best thing is to prepare through fasting over time. Fasting is not just a religious rite but also good for you to relax tension in your stomach. It helps a lot in life. The more you fast, the easier it is to open up yourself to spiritual things and to receive revelation from the spirit realm.

Action Point:

Read and meditate on Proverbs 9.

Take a fast today and break the fast at 6 PM.

10
READING, LEARNING, AND STUDYING

Personal development requires reading for the approval and acceptance of God and men.

"Study and be diligent to show yourself approved to God, a worker who does not need to be ashamed, rightly dividing the word of truth" (2 Timothy 2:15).

The more you study, the more God will use you. Studying is preparation to be qualified for God to use you for your life, your destiny and to making a positive impact on this world.

"To increase your earnings, you must be learning."

"Live as if you were to die tomorrow. Learn as if you were to live forever"—Mahatma Gandhi

A successful person must keep on learning every day and never get tired of learning.

Learning involves having a teachable heart, presenting yourself for teaching, reading, and studying more on your own. Studying is more expansive and involving than just reading. You need to build up yourself.

There was a time the enemies blocked my way from moving forward in life, but I kept on reading the Bible and Christian books, studying, writing, praying, and fasting. And for some years too, my writings could not be published because I had no funds to do that. But when God made the way and opportunities came, I began to publish all the books I had written. Whenever the Enemy says there is a casting down, God says there is a lifting up. "Tough times never lasts but tough people do" – Robert Schuller.

So don't give up. Keep on keeping on. Preparation is a secret to success; the more you prepare, the better your success. Keep on reading, learning, and studying. Live your life based on the Word of God.

Action Point:

Read and meditate on Proverbs 10.
Make sure you are reading a new book at least every week.

11
IDENTIFY YOUR VISION

One of the best factors to success in life is for you to identify your purpose early on and follow it up. Your vision is your dream and your dream is actually your vision. What is your vision for life? Your vision is your future. Your vision is your destiny. Your vision is what you are destined to do in life or what you want at the end of the success. Your vision is what you are pursuing in life. It is a God-given assignment. It is your purpose in life. You are to live each day focusing on your vision. Do not forget it. Make sure you are doing something daily towards the fulfillment of your vision.

"Where there is no vision, the people perish" (Proverbs 29:18).

Martin Luther King Jr. had a dream, which materialized in the long run and it is beneficial to mankind.

"Have a vision, run with the vision, run the race, run with grace."

You have to always keep your dream before you and make sure you are following it up every day. Your dream has to do with your interests, abilities, capabilities and all those things that will make you happy in life. You don't have to pass through this world without fulfilling your dreams (vision). If there are obstacles hindering you, pray them out and go ahead to fulfill your dream. Your dream is your success. It is your destiny. Run after your destiny with singleness of purpose, plans, pursuits, and prayers.

"Don't just have a job to do, but have a purpose in life."

There are lots of distractions in this world that have kept many from fulfilling their destinies. Those distractions are too many now. Be determined to fulfill your vision.

"Your dream is a route to your destiny"

"When you cease to dream you cease to live"
—Malcolm Forbes

Your vision is also your vision in life. Identify and fulfill it. If you don't do the will of God for your life, you will continue to struggle. I pray you will not struggle in vain.

Action Point:

Read and meditate on Proverbs 11

- Receive your purpose in life from God.

- Think about your purpose on the earth.

- Do something about your vision daily.

12
WRITE THE VISION

To keep your vision in your memory, you need to write in a journal and record the ideas and inspirations received. Ideas not written can fly away. Non writing is a form of laziness. Don't be lazy. Write in books and journals; organize your life.

"Then the Lord answered me and said: Write the vision and make it plain on tablets, that he may run who reads it" (Habakkuk 2:2).

Whenever you are thinking, reading, studying, meditating, listening to your mentor or the Holy Spirit, you will learn and receive. As you receive new things from God, the best way to remember is to write them in your journal, jotter or a notebook. As you receive ideas please write them in your journal. Writing helps you retain the idea so it does not fly away as they do if not properly taken care of. The best way to take care of an idea is to write it in a journal or. Not only ideas but also all the good spiritual dreams and vision you have; please write them down and follow up on them as they will unfold and be fulfilled.

Writing also helps you to have a good setting, planning, and preparation before you take action on any ideas or projects. Documenting your thoughts and ideas and planning things to do will make you well coordinated and organized. Therefore, it is very important to have jotters, notes pads, index cards and so on to write and record your thinking, new words, new ideas and what to do.

The more you write, the better you will be at peace. There is no harm in writing. You cannot run everything on your head, please write.

"You fail only if you stop writing" —Ray Bradbury

Action Point:

Read and meditate on Proverbs 12

Write out your vision in life and paste it near your reading table or bedroom.
Get a notebook to write out any new inspirational words or quotes daily.

13
SET GOALS REGULARLY

Goals are signposts to your destination. Having goals in life will help keep you on track and let you know that you are still on the right way to success. Goals are the step-by-step approaches for what you must do to reach success. Goals are those things you have set in line on the path to being successful. So you have to set up your path daily and periodically in life.

Your set-goals will take you to your goals in life, and ultimately, to your destination. You have to set realistic and achievable goals. They are signposts to your destiny.

"For which of you, intending to build a tower, does not sit down first and count the cost, whether he has enough to finish it" (Luke 14:28).

Goal setting can be short term, medium term, long term or for a lifetime. You are to sit down and diligently set all these goals for your life. In the setting of goals, you must be SMART- Specific, Measurable, Action-Oriented, Realistic, and Timely.

"A goal is a dream with a deadline"—Napoleon Hill

Action Point:

Read and meditate on Proverbs 13

Write out your thing to do today and weekly.

14
PLAN TO SUCCEED

"The wise woman builds her house, but the foolish pulls it down with her hands" (Proverbs 14:1).

Somethings you have to do in life and daily are to plan, program, prepare, and pursue your life in the way that God has delivered it to you. You have to focus on what you planned to do with the determination to get to the successful conclusion. The more you plan, the better your life. Don't just dabble into life without planning.

Make a plan. "If you fail to plan, you are planning to fail." You have to make a conscious and deliberate plan on how to fulfill your destiny. The plan you will be making must be in accordance with the purpose of God for your life. Always plan what you are doing well in advance. Everything you need to do tomorrow, write them down the night before. Almighty

God prepared scriptures well in advance, and all the prophecies are happening right before our very eyes.

"A good plan is like a road map: it shows the final destination and usually the best way to get there."—H. Stanley Judd

You only need to put effort and determination into your plans. I was working for a company many years ago as a manager, and I had a secretary. I gave her my list of things to do each morning before I went out to work. She typed them in boldface for me to paste in my bedroom. She actually helped me do it in a beautiful and presentable way but later she said something: "Having all the steps of things to do are very good but in this modern, fast-paced, jet moving, and microwave world who will have the time to do these each day?"

That is the problem with many of us. If you are not patient to do what is needful each time, you might not succeed easily.

Action Point:

Read and meditate on Proverbs 14

Write out your step by step approach to achieve your goals today.

15
TAKE ACTION AND DO IT NOW

Planning and doing nothing about it is vain and creates emptiness in life. You must take positive actions and steps for good results.

One of the principles I learned very well in the United States is "doing." Don't just sit there without doing something. The Americans believe in working and working out ways even where you thought there was no way. They are always on the move and work through 24 hours of the day based on schedules; they plan better ways of doing things to improve every day.

You have to take action in life and on time. Get moving and get going! Nothing moves until you move, and nothing works until you work. Today, find something to do and do it.

When He had stopped speaking, He said to

Simon, Launch out into the deep and let down your nets for a catch.

But Simon answered and said to Him, Master we have toiled all night and caught nothing; nevertheless, at your word I will let down the net.

And when they had done this, they caught a great number of fish, and their net was breaking (Luke 5:4-6)

It has always been said that it is better to try and fail than not trying at all. Take action on your plans and try as much as you can. You will succeed.

"You must do the things you think you cannot do"—Eleanor Roosevelt

If you are too busy to practice these principles, you might not move forward easily. Real success comes only when you invest your time in profitable actions. Don't base your life on the instant microwave mentality of this world. Our God is a God of process. Invest your time wisely.

Action Point:

Read and meditate on Proverbs 15

Take action on your plan today and follow it up.

16
PRAY IT OUT IN FAITH

Praying to God is proof that we have no power of our own, and that we believe only He can do it. To have success in life, you have to pray seriously. Bishop Francis Wale Oke said, "Failure in life is because there is a failure in praying." It is not the will of God for you to fail. However, when praying, you have to pray according to His will. The will of God is the Word of God. Pray whatever the Word says, and you will be a success.

Whatever may be the situation, tell it to Jesus. Pray with the relevant words of faith to your situations, issues, and needs.

"Call unto Me, and I will answer you, and show you great and mighty things, which you do not know" *(Jeremiah 33:3).*

"For assuredly I say unto you, whoever says to this

mountain, be removed and be cast into the sea, and does not doubt in his heart, but believes those things he says will be done, he will have whatever he says. Therefore I say unto you whatever things you ask when you pray, believe that you receive them and you will have them" (Mark 11:23-24).

Prayer is the spiritual force behind your vision. It gives your vision power to materialize. Prayer is a necessity for survival. It is an antidote for affliction. Therefore, make praying your lifestyle.

When you pray, you ask, seek, knock and also make enquiries before you proceed to take steps in doing anything. Make sure you receive answers to your requests before you move ahead in life. Praying is where divinity connects with humanity. Without praying, you might not go far. I pray you will go far.

"God does nothing except in response to believing prayer"—John Wesley

The place of prayer is the secret place of the Most High. It is a place when you shut your door and go into your closet to pray. Continuous and sustained praying can open heaven for you and your loved ones.

Action Point:

Read and meditate on Proverbs 16

Pray for your written vision, goals, and plans that they manifest and be fulfilled.

17
ADD VIGIL

You need to add vigil to your spiritual life. Most quality decisions and upward movements in life are done in the night. God created the heaven and the earth during the night and the results showed in the morning. So for you to have a successful day, you have to vigil in the night.

"God called the light Day, and the darkness He called Night. So the evening and the morning were the first day" (Genesis 1:5).

Vigil is one of the spices you add to your spiritual life. Praying in the night is a secret weapon for new creation and transformation. That is when you can call those things that were not as if they were. It is also a time to effectively battle the enemies. When Paul and Silas prayed and sang in the night, the prison doors were opened by supernatural means. So by praying in the night, you can provoke the angels of God to come to your rescue.

Action Point:

Read and meditate on Proverbs 17

Do a praise and prayer vigil today starting from 11:45 PM to 12:30 AM minimum

18
THINK BIG AND CONFESS POSITIVELY

God used His Word to frame and create the world. The Word that you speak will go into the space and accomplish whatever you send it to do. Therefore, speak positive words to your life and every situation. Confessing the Word brings powerful effects. And it is more rewarding to personalize these words when confessing them.

"But what does it say? 'The word is near you, in your mouth and in your heart' (that is the word of faith which we preach):That if you confess with your mouth the Lord Jesus and believe in your heart that God raised Him from the dead, you will be saved" (Roman 10:8-9).

"Optimism is the faith that leads to achievement. Nothing can be done without hope or confidence" —Helen Keller

Begin today to think the way God thinks. Think big, think increase, think possibility. If you have positive words in your heart, your inner being will be good and will produce correct outward results.

"For as he thinks in his heart, so is he" (Proverbs 23:7).

What you think is what you speak. So think positively every time and every moment of your life. Wait to see the positive results and help coming your way.

"For out of the abundance of the heart the mouth speaks" (Matthew 12:34).

So, therefore, store positive words in your heart by reading, hearing, and listening to the positive encouraging words from great men of God. The quality of your thinking depends on the quality of information you stored in your heart.

"Change your thought and you change your world" —Norman Vincent Peale

Faith is believing what the Word says without doubt in your heart. Faith in God usually works even when the anointing is not present to work. The anointing is usually given to bless others but you need faith in the Word of God to bless yourself. "Healer, heal thyself." The healer can heal himself by exercising faith in the Word of God. However, he can use both the faith and the anointing to heal others.

Therefore, you need to develop and increase your faith in God by praying, totally trusting Him, relying on Him, believing in what the Word says and confessing them into your life. As you do these, you will be graduating to the next level on the ladder of faith. Possibility thinking is believing that with God, all things are possible. So think big and confess positively the word of faith.

Confession requires you to speak your beliefs, your wants or your future aloud with your mouth.

Action Point:

Read and meditate on Proverbs 18

Begin to say positive affirmations about your goals and vision

19
IMAGINE AND VISUALIZE

Imagination is putting an abstract picture of what you want before you. Imagination gives you good pictures of the results you are expecting. You have to visualize the good picture, which the heavens will surely supply. This is also a very powerful spiritual aspect of your life. The more you visualize, the more the Holy Spirit will have materials to work with.

"Looking unto Jesus, the author and finisher of our faith, who for the joy that was set before Him endured the cross, despising the shame, and has sat down at the right hand of the throne of God" (Hebrews 12:2).

One of the ways to secure a better future is to travel, be exposed, and visit new places. Your imagination and visualization will then be well developed. It will consist of all that you have been seeing in life and your preferred expectation.

You need to visit various places like big stores, malls, rivers, zoos, flowers, plants, colors, parks and other monumental buildings and sites throughout the world. Or you can view these places in magazines or internet websites. All these will help you in your imagination to prepare a better future for yourself.

All things bright and beautiful
All creatures great and small
All things wise and wonderful
The Lord God made them all.

Cecil F. Alexander

Putting a picture of what you want or where you are going before you will keep you focused in life and avoid distractions.

"Everything you can imagine is real" – Pablo Picasso

Action Point:

Read and meditate on Proverbs 19

Get a pictorial representation of your vision in a paper form and paste it where you can see it daily.

20
WORK AND SET UP YOUR BUSINESS

There is a time for everything. This is called time management. There is a time to work; there is a time to play, and there a is time to pray. Work while you work; play when to play, and pray when to pray. This is the beginning of success. Work doesn't kill. You have to work to fulfill your dreams and vision. However, one of the best works to do is that which aligns with your vision and dreams or leads you to have your own business and fulfill your dreams.

"Living without working is dying without knowing."

To be fruitful, you must be productive. You can work for an individual or a company or start your own business as God has given you power. As you work, do the kind of job that interests you and makes you happy, which also allows you to use your God-given skills, gifts, and talents to better the world.

"Then the Lord God took the man and put him in the garden of Eden to tend keep it" (Genesis 2:15).

"For even when we were with you, we commanded you this: if anyone will not work, neither shall he eat" (2 Thessalonians 3:10).

When you work, you will have money to eat, take care of many things, save, and fulfill your vision. A lazy man doesn't like to work. Work, don't be lazy and do not steal (Ephesians 4:28). It is either you work to collect a salary or create your own business to generate an income for you. Whichever you do, make sure the income is enough to let you fulfill your vision and purpose in life. Pursue your purpose and work on your dreams and projects. You are a success!

"In all labor there is profit, but idle chatter leads only to poverty" (Proverbs 14:23).

All the above scriptures point to the fact that work is not a punishment but a means to build your life.

"Nothing works until you work."

"The only place where success comes before work is in dictionary"—Vidal Sassoon

Invest in your future by pursuing your God-given dreams and completing your projects. You must make an impact on this world and prepare for your future. You must go after your dreams in life.

"Jesus said to them, My food is to do the will of Him who sent Me, and to finish His work" (John 4:34).

You can work for or work with anybody or organization but when the time comes, do not forget any of your dreams or projects. Do them, pursue them, and make hay while the sun shines.

You have to fulfill your dream because it is your destiny.

"All our dreams can come true if we have the courage to pursue them"—Walt Disney

Action Point:

Read and meditate on Proverbs 20

Think and plan on setting up your own business or how to improve the existing one.

21
BRING YOUR FIRSTFRUITS

The first income in your work or business or in a new year belongs to God, not your parents because God is first. Bringing your firstfruit is a commandment you have to obey.

"The priest shall wave them with the bread of the firstfruits as a wave offering before the Lord, with the two lambs. They shall be holy to the Lord for the priest" (Leviticus 23:20).

Firstfruits, tithing, and giving qualify you to recognize God as the giver of all good things (James 1:17). And in your appreciation, you have to give your first back to Him (Matthew 6:33). Whatever we give to Him, He will surely repay us manifold. When you give, you will receive more (Luke 6:38). Bringing your firstfruits is evidence that you recognize God as the source of all blessings.

"Honor the Lord with you possessions, and with the firstfruits of all your increase; so your barns will be filled with plenty" (Proverbs 3:9-10).

Honoring the Lord with your firstfruits makes Him first in your life. If you always receive without giving or releasing back to the system of God, you will begin to go down and eventually dry up. I pray that will not be your portion. Giving firstfruits and tithes are means for us not to dwindle in life. That is the system of God.

In history and in all my life, I have never seen one dead person take any of his money and properties to heaven or hell. But the more you give and spread what God gave you to better His agenda, the more treasures will be waiting for you in heaven (Matthew 6:23-32). Giving is a means of transferring our treasures to heaven (money transfer). Somebody said when you pay your bills first, you are not making God first in your life. Firstfruits, tithes, and giving belong to the house of God. Don't query it.

Mr. Moses and Mr. David on separate occasions in the United States got approval for their car purchases on credit even though from all indications, they were not qualified. But after bringing their firstfruits into the house of God, God moved on their behalf. As you bring in your own firstfruits into the house of God, God will move on your behalf, making impossibility possible.

"Make God first priority. He's worth it" — Monica Johnson

Action Point:

Read and meditate on Proverbs 21

Make a habit of paying your firstfruits of a new year, new job or new business to your pastor

22
BRING GOD'S TITHE

You are not paying your tithe but you must bring God's tithe. The money belongs to God from the onset long before you start your work or business. He is the owner of everything, and He is giving you the opportunity to earn on the condition that you will bring His share of the income, which is just ten percent.

Will a man rob God? Yet you have robbed me! But you say, in what way have we robbed you? In tithes and offering. You are cursed with a curse, for you have robbed Me, even this whole nation. Bring all the tithes into the storehouse, that there may be food in My house, and try Me now in this, says the Lord of hosts, if I will not open for you the windows of heaven and pour out for you such blessings that there will not be enough room to receive it. And I will rebuke devourer for your sakes, so that he will not destroy the fruit of your ground, nor shall the vine fail to bear fruit for you in the field, says the Lord of hosts; and all the nations will call you blessed, for you will be a delightful land, says the Lord of hosts (Malachi 3:8-12).

"And all the tithes of the land, whether of the seed of the land or of the fruit of the tree, is the Lord's. It is holy to the Lord" (Leviticus 27:30).

Tithing is a secret to ending poverty. If God is first in your life then pay God's tithe first before you start spending your income. Many are having ups and downs because they are not consistent in paying God's tithe.

"One of the blessings that come from paying a full tithing is developing faith to live an even higher law. To live in the celestial kingdom, we must live the law of consecration. There we must be able to feel that all we are and all we have belong to God."—Henry B. Eyring

A brother in New York was being faithful in his tithe payment to God. In his working place as a real estate official, he began to bring in good sales and to close new deals, which increased his income dramatically. He became the envy of his colleagues who did not know his secrets. He eventually told them it was the power of tithing that was working for him. This power and obedience to tithing are greater than any charm or juju. Because with tithing, God will protect, preserve, and bless you, but He will also rebuke the devourer for your sake.

Consistent giving and regular tithing in the kingdom of God is a solution to financial crisis.

Action Point:

Read and meditate on Proverbs 22

- Don't forget to bring in God's tithes promptly.

- Pay tithes on any increase or income, whether gifts or inheritance.

23
SAVE FOR THE FUTURE

The real way to have money is to keep money. You don't have to spend all your money. You need to save part of it. What happens when what you have is not even enough? The rule is to learn how to save and keep on saving to have more money whenever you need it in the future. In any case, there is never a time when what you have will be enough. We always want more.

So you have to practice saving money as a habit for life. The more you are faithful in saving, the more financial breakthroughs you will have. And the earlier, the better you start off in life. Saving is a form of discipline and self-control. If you can't save your money, it shows clearly that you are not financially disciplined. You have to do this by yourself. It is your responsibility and you must be responsible in life.

Pay yourself first. Set aside some money for yourself, your children, emergencies, your projects and for your future. Don't be a beggar when you are old. Saving money requires a lot of discipline. The more you save your money, the more disciplined you are.

"Go to the ant, you sluggard! Consider her ways and be wise, which, having no captain, overseer or ruler, provides her supplies in the summer, and gathers her food in the harvest" (Proverbs 6:6-8).

Until you save your money, you cannot be saved from poverty. Save your money and invest your savings.

"If saving money is wrong, I don't want to be right" —William Shatner

I taught this principle to a church pastored by my friend in Ogun state, Nigeria. At the end of the teaching, the man of God was astonished and began the practice. Within a short period of time, he had some money in his savings, which boosted his financial power. And at the same time, God began to show up for him. If you lift up your hands, God will lift you up.

The secret to saving is discipline and determination. Until you save your money, you cannot have a financial breakthrough.

Action Point:

Read and meditate on Proverbs 23

- Make a habit of saving a certain percentage for yourself for life.

- Also, keep some of your extra change, notes, and coins in a local bank like a piggy bank in your home.

24
INVEST AND SOW INTO THE KINGDOM

There is a principle that says pay yourself first. That is your special saving. This saving is meant for investment to generate other income for further reinvestment. Challenges might come and emergencies may arise but never ever touch your savings that are meant for investment. There are two kinds of investments: the one you invest in businesses and the other you invest in the kingdom of God.

Investment opportunities will work for you and will generate lots of other income for you whether you are awake or sleeping. Investment is a wealth system that will bring in other income to you. You have to work, get to this level and keep on investing. It is when you get to this level that you will be sure of some securities in the future. To be on the right track, please get expert advice on investing. Buying and consuming will not bring you additional income. It is investing your savings in other sources that will bring you more income. So start investing today. Trust God with your finances and material blessings.

On the other hand, investing in the things of God is putting your treasures where moth and thieves will never enter. It works better than shares, stocks or real estate. The enemies cannot attack it. It is a sure protection and yields higher returns. It works. If you support what God is doing, He will bless you beyond measure.

"Do not lay up for yourself treasures on earth, where moth and rust destroy and where thieves break in and steal; but lay up for yourselves treasures in heaven, where neither moth nor rust destroys and where thieves do not break in and steal. For where your treasure is, there your heart will be also" (Matthew 6:19-21).

"But seek first the kingdom of God and His righteousness, and all these things shall be added to you" (Matthew 6:33).

If you seek the things of God first, He will always be there for you

"God comes first. Paradise is not cheap"—
Hakeem Olajuwon

A sister in Boston sowed to a man of God then God opened doors of opportunities for her. She got a cool and comfortable job and all other things began to work in her favor.

As you too apply this principle, you will succeed.

Action Point:

Read and meditate on Proverbs 24

- Take a certain amount and sow it into the life of a man of God.

- Give also to support the work of God-like projects, missions, and evangelism.

25
CARE FOR YOUR FAMILY

It is your responsibility to take care of your family. Do not neglect or abandon this. Work hard and do your duty. Be responsible in life.

"Do not look upon me, because I am dark, because the sun has tanned me. My mother's sons were angry with me; they made me keeper of the vineyards, but my own vineyard I have not kept" (Song of Solomon 1:6).

"But if anyone does not provide for his own, and especially for those of his household, he has denied the faith and is worse than an unbeliever" (1 Timothy 5:8).

You have to keep your own vineyard; you have to provide for your immediate family.

Caring for your family is the highest form of responsibility in life. It is one of your assignments and priorities from God.

"I constantly work at balance. For me, my family comes first. If my family is taken care of, then everything else usually falls into place"
—Faith Hill

Action Point:

Read and meditate on Proverbs 25

- Stay with your family at home today or buy gifts for all of them.

- Help your kids to cross check their homework and play with them.

26
GIVE AND GIVE CONTINUOUSLY

"Give, and it will be given unto you: good measure, pressed down, shaken together, and running over will be put into your bosom. For with the same measure that you use, it will be measured back to you" (Luke 6:38).

Y ou are to give to the following:

Give to the Work of God

To give to the work of God, you have to believe in God. The more you believe, the more your benefits. You can give to God through gospels, projects, missions, and every other thing that supports the kingdom of God.

"Hear me O Judah and you inhabitants of Jerusalem: believe in the Lord your God, and you shall be established; believe His prophets, and you shall prosper" (2 Chronicles 20:20).

Give to Your Pastors

"Hear me O Judah and you inhabitants of Jerusalem: believe in the Lord your God, and you shall be established; believe His prophets, and you shall prosper" (2 Chronicles 20:20).

"He who receives a prophet in the name of a prophet shall receive the prophet's reward, and he who receives a righteous man in the name of a righteous man shall receive a righteous man's reward" (Matthew 10:41).

Give to Your Parents

"Children obey your parents in the Lord, for this is right. Honor your father and mother, which is the first commandment with promise: that it may be well with you and you may live long on earth" (Ephesians 6:1-3).

Give to the Poor

"He who has pity on the poor lends to the Lord, and He will pay back what he has given" (Proverbs 19:17).

True happiness and fulfillment come when you give your time, talents, treasures, and resources to others. Live to give and give to live. You cannot out-give a giver. Jesus said in Acts 20:35, "It is more blessed to give than to receive." So give more to receive more blessings. Give your time, talents, treasures, and resources. Giving is a secret to receiving.

"Success is finding satisfaction in giving a little more than you take" —Christopher Reeve

If you can give anything to God, He will give anything to you. Giving is an opportunity to change your level.

Action Point:

Read and meditate on Proverbs 26

Give monthly to all the above-mentioned groups of people.

27
OWE NO ONE

A borrower is a servant to the lender. God does not want you to be in debt. When you borrow, you are in a pit, and it might take a long time for you to get back on level ground. Borrowing can bring backwardness, depression, shame, and disrespect.

"Owe no one anything except to love one another, for he who loves another has fulfilled the law" (Romans 13:8).

"You shall lend to many nations, but you shall not borrow" (Deuteronomy 28:12e).

"The rich rules over the poor, and borrower is servant to the lender" (Proverbs 22:7).

"People should watch out for three things: avoid a major addiction, don't get so deeply into debt that it control your life, and don't start a family before you are ready to settle down"—James Taylor

Try as much as possible not to borrow or be in debt. The truth is that borrowing is not the will of God for your life. The promise of God for us is to lend to nations, communities, and organizations. If you continue borrowing, you have placed yourself to be a servant in that respect.

Pay up all your debts. Do not borrow except on rare occasions when you have the means to easily pay off what you owe.

Action Point:

Read and meditate on Proverbs 27

- Pay your debts.

- Avoid any new debts.

28
OBEY AND DO THE RIGHT THING

Righteousness is doing the right thing at the right time. When you do the right thing, you will be at the right place to receive the right blessings.

"But you O man of God flees these things and pursue righteousness, godliness, faith, love, patient, gentleness, gentleness" (1 Timothy 6:11).

Obedience is heeding to the voice of God, the Holy Spirit and your decision towards your vision in life.

Obedience is a single word for you to receive blessings from God (Deuteronomy 28:1, John 2:5). Obedience is doing exactly what God asked you to do. Partial obedience is disobedience; delayed obedience is disobedience. God requires prompt and total obedience. Abraham obeyed God without even knowing the land he was going to. Obedience attracts blessings to you. The more you obey God, the more your blessings. Until you obey God, you won't have breakthrough in life. Obey God and leave the rest to Him.

"So Samuel said: has the Lord as great delight in burnt offerings and sacrifices, as in obeying the voice of the Lord? Behold, to obey is better than sacrifice, and to heed than he fat of rams" (1 Samuel 15:22).

"Do the right thing, it will gratify some people and astonish the rest" —Mark Twain

The only way to be righteous is to obey God.

Action Point:

Read and meditate on Proverbs 28

- Obey the Word of God.

- Obey the voice of the Holy Spirit.

- Obey your mentor.

29
BE SECRETIVE

It is not everything you are doing that you must tell everybody. Know what to say at any particular point in time. You only communicate with people who have good intentions for you. If you share your vision with some people, they will be angry and look for ways to discourage you or frustrate your efforts. Go and learn from Joseph in Genesis Chapter 37.

"And Hezekiah was attentive to them, and showed them all the house of his treasures the silver and gold, the spices and precious ointment, and all his armory — all that was found among his treasures. There was nothing in his house or in all his dominion that Hezekiah did not show them" (2 Kings 20:13).

I was unable to get some success early in life because of household enemies. The household enemies are the people who are very close to you. They know you in and out. We all have a lot of them. Before you make any move they already know.

It took me several years to realize that you cannot share your vision with everyone. Even when I discovered this truth and began to apply it, the enemies were still angry with me and started to monitor all my activities with the intention to prevent, disrupt, and discourage me. You have to be wise in your dealings with people. The best way to do that is to speak less and do more.

Make sure you complete what you are doing before you tell most people. Doing this will guarantee you success in life. The same enemies will help you to be more determined and get to your destination.

"Do not trust in a friend; do not put confidence in a companion; guard the doors of your mouth from her who lies in your bosom. For son dishonors father, daughters rises against her mother, daughter-in-law against her mother-in-law; a man's enemies are the men of his own household" (Micah 7:5-6).

You are not obliged to tell everyone your secrets.

"The most successful company on Silicon Valley is Apple, and they are the most secretive" —Carol Bartz.

I told a woman not to talk too much about her life to everyone. She was angry at the way I presented it because I said she talked too much. But eventually, she changed, keeping her plans to herself until they materialized. Within a short period of time, she got her citizenship and her daughter entered the States with ease.

To be successful, you have to be secretive.

Action Point:

Read and meditate on Proverbs 29

- Keep your vision to yourself until it matures.

- Don't be a talkative.

30
CHARACTER AND ATTITUDE

Living uprightly and in holiness is a continuous effort on your part. This will make it impossible for the enemies to attack you.

"There was a man in the land of Uz, whose name was Job: and that was blameless and upright, and one who fear God and shunned evil" (Job 1:1).

"The man of upright life has a guiltless heart, frees from all dishonest or thought of vanity" —Thomas Carlyle

Good character sustains your integrity for life. It is your responsibility to behave or misbehave yourself. A child of God without character will end up in a mess. You have a right to choose to move away from what is ungodly even in this present world.

"Far be it from me that I should say you are right; till I die I will not put away my integrity from me" (Job 27:5).

"Integrity is doing the right thing, even when no one is watching" —C.S. Lewis

Live upright and be faithful. Develop good character and integrity.

Attitude has to do with the way you react when something or nothing happens. Attitude is your disposition in life. The best attitude is to be optimistic and always finding a better way of doing things. A good attitude will make you develop positively each day. The Bible says, "Be angry but sin not." That is an attitude. Your attitude will determine your altitude. That is a lifting, a promotion in life. However, it is only a positive attitude that will promote you.

"But what do you think? A man had two sons, and he came to the first and said, son, go, work today in my vineyard. He answered and said, I will not, but afterward he regretted it and went. Then he came to the second and said likewise. And he answered and said, I go, sir, but he did not go" (Matthew 21:28-30).

"Your attitude will determine your altitude in life"

You need to possess and show positive attitudes all the time. Someone said: "Happiness is a choice." Therefore I say choose happiness. There are many types of attitudes. The way you react or respond to a situation will determine whether you can control it or not. You might not be able to control every situation but you can control your reaction. For example, if someone makes you angry, you might choose not to be angry. Also, in whatever situation, praise the Lord. An attitude of praise will elevate you in life.

"People may hear your words, but they feel your attitude" —John C. Maxwell

Action Point:

Read and meditate on Proverbs 30

- Take your time before you react to any issue

- Be upright in all your ways

31
BE THANKFUL

One of the best principles of life is to thank God always. You are to thank Him whether you are in a good or bad situation. We should learn how to be thankful in all our doings because God created us, and we are alive to praise Him. One of our functions in life and even in heaven is to praise God. Don't be ungrateful in life. Be thankful for all the people He is bringing your way. Be joyful, be happy, and be grateful. Happiness is a choice; therefore, choose to be happy and thank God at each moment of your life. When you complain, you are not appreciating God for your life. Have an attitude of gratitude, live a life of gratitude. Be grateful to God. Appreciate others and be thankful to them. Praising God is a way to be thankful to Him.

"Let everything that has breath praise the Lord. Praise the Lord" (Psalms 150:6).

A great man of God in Ibadan, Nigeria started thanking God in prayer from 10.00 AM till 10.00 PM. At the end of the day, he had a great victory in his personal life. Thanking God produces other tangible expectations.

"A thankful heart is a merry heart."

Apart from thanking God, we have to be grateful for people who help or work with us both at home and the workplace. Just make a decision to say, "Thank you."

"Thank you is the best prayer that anyone could say. I say that a lot. Thank you expresses gratitude, humility and understanding"—Alice Walker

The will of the Enemy is to steal, kill, and destroy. For each moment, the Enemy does not want a bit of success for you. He is always angry and bitter in his heart and looks for ways to harm you. But because God has kept you this far and against all the wickedness, I think this is cause for thanksgiving and appreciation. The more you thank God, the more He will move to perform better things in your life and to fulfill all the promises He has for you. Why don't you create a special way to praise, thank and appreciate God today?

Action Point:

Read and meditate on Proverbs 31

Sing unto the Lord the joyful songs and praise His name

SOME RECOMMENDED BOOKS TO READ

The following books are highly recommended for you on your journey of success in life. Most of them were first published in the 1900s. They must be in your library.

- Think and Grow Rich by Napoleon Hill
- Tough Times Never Last but Tough People Do by Robert Schuller
- The Richest Man in Babylon by George S. Clason
- As He Thinks in His Heart by James Allen
- Acres of Diamond by Russell Conwell
- It Works – the famous little red book that makes your dream come true by RHJ
- The Strangest Secret by Earl Nightingale
- Your Invisible Power by Genevieve Behrend
- The Anointing by Kenneth Hagin
- The Hidden Power of Prayer and Fasting by Mahesh Chavda

ABOUT THE AUTHOR

Reverend Olatunji Joseph Ogunbanjo is the founder, president, and senior pastor of Christ Light Affairs International Ministries (CLAIM), worldwide. He is anointed to teach, train, and disciple individuals and nations to fulfill their destinies in life and ministries. He believes that success is for all the children of God, and it is obtainable through discovery in God's Word.

Olatunji started his ministries in 2003; he was appointed as a pastor in 2004. He obtained a Post Graduate Diploma in 2006 from the Redeemed Christian Bible College, Lagos, Nigeria. He was ordained a pastor in April 2006 from his former church. His ministries were commissioned and inaugurated in September 2008 and since then he has been building successful Christians in life and ministries throughout the world. He was ordained a Reverend by Bishop Francis Wale Oke of the Sword of the Spirit Ministries, Ibadan, Nigeria in September 2009.

Olatunji also holds Certificates Courses in Leadership from Daystar Leadership Academy, Nigeria and Word of Faith Bible Institute of Winners Chapel, Nigeria. Olatunji is highly sought after speaker for seminars, conferences, and churches. He preaches with anointing and the power of the Holy Ghost with miracles, signs, and wonders following. He is presently in the United States of America on a mission doing exploits for God.

www.ingramcontent.com/pod-product-compliance
Lightning Source LLC
Chambersburg PA
CBHW060946040426
42445CB00011B/1028